Yosemite
Topropes

by Rob Floyd

Yosemite Topropes

by Rob Floyd

ISBN # 1-892540-05-3

For a complete list of titles available from Sharp End Publishing, please write to P.O. Box 1613, Boulder, CO 80306-1613 or e.mail us at inforock@aol.com.

Sharp End Publishing is always looking for new material. Please send queries to the address or e.mail address above.

Cover photos by Chris Falkenstein, Falkfoto

READ THIS BEFORE USING THIS GUIDE BOOK

Rock climbing, including toproping, is extremely dangerous. A small and incomplete list of possible dangers include: loose rock, weather, anchor failure (fixed anchors, natural anchors, and removable protection), dangerous pendulums, equipment failure, etc.

THE AUTHOR AND PUBLISHER EXPRESSLY DISCLAIM ALL REPRESENTATIONS AND WARRANTIES REGARDING THIS GUIDE, THE ACCURACY OF THE INFORMATION CONTAINED HEREIN, AND THE RESULTS OF YOUR USE HEREOF, INCLUDING WITHOUT LIMITATION, IMPLIED WARRANTIES OF MERCHANTABILITY AND FITNESS FOR A PARTICULAR PURPOSE. THE USER ASSUMES ALL RISK ASSOCIATED WITH THE USE OF THIS GUIDE.

It is your responsibility to take care of yourself while climbing. Seek a professional instructor or guide if you are unsure of your ability to handle any circumstances that may arise. This guide is not intended as an instructional manual.

Table of Contents

This guide is not intended as an instructional manual. While toproping may be safer than other manifestations of rock climbing, it is still a dangerous endeavor requiring knowhow and experience. The information in this guide will help steer experienced climbers to toproping opportunities in what is arguably the world's most magnificent climbing area.

This guidebook relies on the use of icons to indicate the difficulty of the approach, the angle of the route, difficulty reaching the toprope anchor, gear requirements, and child safety at the base.

Approach Information

 Easy Approach: Less than 10 minutes and/or easy hiking.

 Moderate Approach: 15-30 minutes and/or some steep terrain.

 Difficult Approach: An hour or more of hiking and/or steep terrain.

Anchor Information

 Natural Anchors: Nearby trees and/or boulders make suitable anchors. Back up with gear when possible.

 Gear Anchors: Bring your own pro to set up anchors.

 Bolt Anchors: Bolts are in place. Know how to judge their safety and back them up when possible.

Child Safety Information

 Kids Safe: Nature of the crag lends itself to being relatively safe for kids.

 Kids Unsafe: Loose rock or unstable talus create dangers for children. Proximity to road may also be a factor.

Anchor Access Information

 Easy Access: Top of the crag and/or anchors are easily accessible with nothing more than a short hike.

 Moderate Access: Some scrambling may be necessary to reach the top and/or the anchors.

 Difficult Access: At least 3rd class and sometimes 4th class scrambling required to reach the top. Belays recommended. Rappels may be involved.

Rock Angle Information

 Slabby Climbing: Routes tend to be on rock less than 90 degrees.

 Vertical Climbing: Routes tend to be vertical in nature.

 Steep Climbing: Routes tend to be overhanging.

Child Safety Note:
Parents should check out the cliff in advance and evaluate the safety of the surroundings, as the nature of crags is generally unsafe.

Introduction

Yosemite is the Disneyland of rock climbing: complete with tourists galore, pizza and beer, souvenir shops, ice cream parlors, overly friendly bears, squirrels and birds. Like the Magic Kingdom, the Valley offers countless exciting rides. The Nose on El Capitan is the premiere E-ticket ride, but for those who seek tamer terrain, this guide highlights quality A-ticket topropes.

Many visiting climbers arrive in Yosemite with limited racks, families, or with other activities in mind. "Where can I toprope?" is a question frequently posed to rangers and fellow climbers. *Yosemite Topropes* compiles a list of the best toprope problems in the Valley, drawing largely on cliffs that contain a concentration of toprope routes. Icons will help climbers discern which cliff best suits their agenda.

Though toproping can be safer than embarking on the sharp end, don't be lulled into a false sense of security—many dangers accompany rock climbing in the Valley.

Some safety considerations that need to be addressed are as follows. Rockfall is a real danger. (My 200 foot rope is now a 145 foot rope due to this natural occurrence). Be extra careful not to knock any rocks off when scrambling around the tops of cliffs, and conversely, keep aware of potential rockfall from above. Also, the moss and lichen that covers much of the granite slabs gets extremely slick and slippery when wet. If it rains even a little, be extra cautious walking or scrambling on lichen-covered rock. While all the precautions of toproping in other environments must be observed, one problem characteristic of the Valley is the presence of aluminum rappel rings. Many of them are hollow and can burn through from the friction caused by toproping. Instead, toprope directly from anchors and multiple locking carabiners. *Yosemite Topropes* isn't, by any stretch, an instructional guide, so I won't get carried away with advice. If you're in doubt, hire a professional guide. Two final notes: Yosemite is full of poison oak. If you don't know what it looks like, familiarize yourself with it before you head out to climb, and always keep a keen eye open for rattlesnakes. I saw two of them during my most recent visit.

Be safe and have fun.

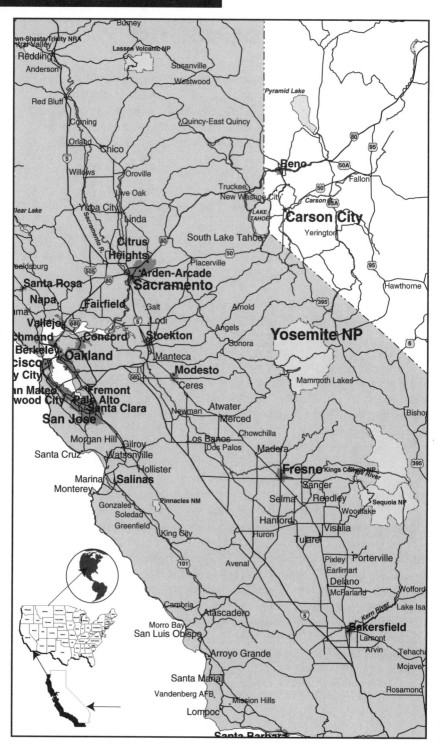

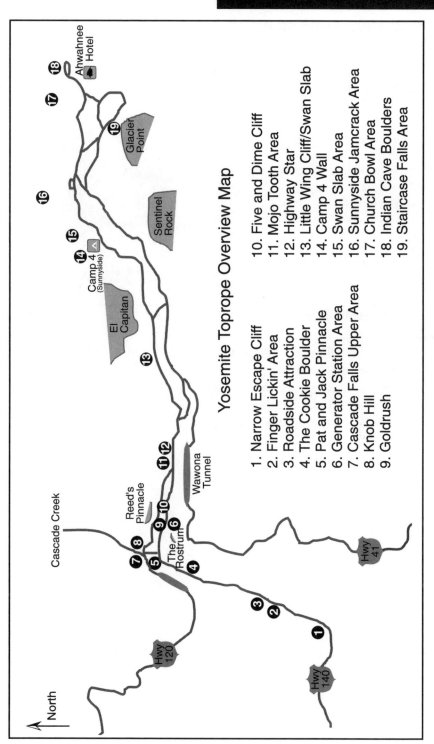

Yosemite Toprope Overview Map

1. Narrow Escape Cliff
2. Finger Lickin' Area
3. Roadside Attraction
4. The Cookie Boulder
5. Pat and Jack Pinnacle
6. Generator Station Area
7. Cascade Falls Upper Area
8. Knob Hill
9. Goldrush
10. Five and Dime Cliff
11. Mojo Tooth Area
12. Highway Star
13. Little Wing Cliff/Swan Slab
14. Camp 4 Wall
15. Swan Slab Area
16. Sunnyside Jamcrack Area
17. Church Bowl Area
18. Indian Cave Boulders
19. Staircase Falls Area

North

Cascade Creek

Hwy 120

Hwy 41

Hwy 140

Reed's Pinnacle

The Rostrum

Wawona Tunnel

El Capitan

Camp 4 (Sunnyside)

Sentinel Rock

Glacier Point

Ahwahnee Hotel

NARROW ESCAPE CLIFF

This cliff is located on the north side of Highway 140, 1.0 mile west of the Arch Rock Entrance Station. It's easily detected by locating the prominent rock overhanging the road and then hiking due north from there. This area is a good place to practice the dark craft of offwidth climbing.

1. A Desperate Kneed
5.11a
Put your OW skills to the test on this four-inch leftmost crack.

2. Narrow Escape 5.10c
Thrash, battle, and scratch your way up the nine-inch crack just right of 1.

3. Remember Ribbon Falls 5.12
Climb the steep, thin crack in the alcove.

FINGER LICKIN' AREA

A grievous approach through thick poison oak yields stellar splitter cracks. One mile east from the Arch Rock Entrance Station hike straight up to a power pole and then follow the trail NE. This will bring you to the base of Snatch Power. To reach the anchors, scramble up 20 feet left of Petty Larceny. For the easiest exit, rap off Jawbone when you're done climbing.

1. Petty Larceny 5.11+
Hard down low to great hand jams.
A little dirty.
2. Snatch Power 5.10c
Climb the thin crack then punch through a difficult roof to an off-hands lieback.
3. Jaw Bone 5.10a
The spectacular off-hands "S" crack.

ROADSIDE ATTRACTION

This area offers difficult crack climbing located within mere spitting distance of the road. Park at the split boulder on the south side of Highway 140, 1.1 miles east of the Arch Rock Entrance Station. Roadside Attraction is across the road and 25 yards east. If you've ever wondered what 5.12 crack climbing feels like, your opportunity awaits.

1. Roadside Attraction 5.12a
Technical stemming up the dihedral leads to the perfect finger crack.

2. Roadside Infarction 5.12b
Climb the desperately flaring finger crack to the roof.

3. Back to the Future 5.12b
Michael J. Fox is rumored to have first freed this super-steep finger crack 100 yards up and right of 2.

THE COOKIE BOULDER

This is the huge white boulder located in the river just below the Cookie Cliff 0.5 mile down from the Cascade Falls Bridge. Back up the anchor for 3 with the anchors for 1 and 2.

1. Unknown 5.11
The leftmost dihedral.
2. Unknown 5.11
Head up the right dihedral.
3. Unknown 5.9-5.10
(depending on eliminates)
Climb the overhanging jugs and slopers to the top.

PAT AND JACK PINNACLE

This awesome area is located directly west of the Cascade Falls Bridge. Park at the picnic area 50 yards past the bridge, cross the road and head straight up to the wall via a climber's trail. This trail will spit you out at the Sherrie's Crack area near the west end of the wall. To reach the anchors of Sherrie's Crack, hike up about 100 feet left, scramble over to the big tree above, and rap down to the top of Sherrie's Crack. Rigging this toprope could be the crux of the climb but it's worth the extra effort.

1. Sherrie's Crack 5.10c
Every crack should be this fine. Dicey fingers, to bomber hands, to pumper underclings.
2. Unknown 5.10+
Climb through the thin crux of Sherrie's Crack, turn the corner, and head up the face past a line of bolts on the left.
3. Nurdle 5.8
Cruise along the angling crack just right of Sherrie's Crack.
4. Knob Job 5.10
The beautiful double crack system right of Nurdle.

GENERATOR STATION AREA

 This area hosts easy to set up topropes on four different boulders near the old generator station on Highway 140, approximately 1.2 miles west of the Hwy120/Hwy140 junction.

1. Generator Crack 5.10c
This is the enormous west-facing crack on the boulder at the gate. A truly heinous offwidth.

2. Conductor Crack 5.10d
The cool finger crack directly across the road from the gate.

3. The Blade 5.12
Knife through the right-angling finger crack for 30 feet. Fifty yards NE of the previous route.

4. The Gauntlet 5.11
Go to war on the off-hands overhang 10 feet right of The Blade.

CASCADE FALLS UPPER AREA

This area is located where Highway 120 crosses Cascade Creek, beneath the Cascade Falls Bridge. You can see these less than stellar climbs in their spectacular setting from the bridge.

1. On The Spot 5.11
Climb the face past a bolt to gain a large lieback. *Use a directional to avoid swinging into the dihedral.*

2. Cascade Crack 5.10
Only during low water can you start this fist crack.

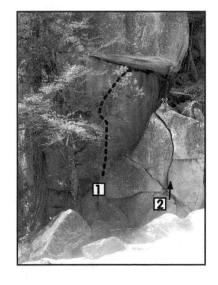

KNOB HILL

Interested in fun slab climbing on cool knobs and cracks? Then go here.
Park across the highway at the Cascade Bridge Parking area on Highway
120 and hike up the steep climber's trail to the right. You'll need two cords
to toprope 3-5. Scramble up a steep dirt gully just to their left to get to the
anchor.

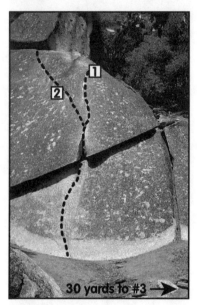

30 yards to #3 →

1. Pot Belly 5.7

Scratch through a tricky crux down low then move into a superb finger
crack.

2. Unknown 5.9

Same start as for Pot Belly but head into the left crack.

3. Movin' To Montana 5.8

Climb the fun knob and bolt-infested slab.

4. Sloth Wall 5.7

Begin in the crack just right of 3, then continue along to finish on the
knobs.

5. Anti-Ego Crack 5.7

Start 20 feet right of 4, head up the crack and finish on the knob-covered
slab. *Use a directional near the top to avoid a body crushing swing.*

(continued from previous page)

6. Turkey Pie 5.7

Gobble up the right-angling lieback to the perfect hand crack. *Again, use a directional to avoid a swing down low.*

GOLDRUSH

This is the obvious climb near the east end of the tunnel just west of Reeds Pinnacle. This stout overhanging crack is a must for anyone wanting to power through burly fist jams.

1. Goldrush 5.11+

The obvious fist crack by the tunnel.

Gold Rush

FIVE AND DIME CLIFF

This awesome cliff is accessed by parking at Reeds Pinnacle (the large parking area between the two short tunnels on Highway 120) and hiking down the trail on the uphill end of the eastern tunnel. The top of this cliff is easily accessed from this trail as well as the base. Besides the routes pictured, there are three easily toproped sport climbs in the 5.10 range to the left of Chump Change.

1. Chump Change 5.12a
Success will not come cheap on this stellar finger crack that leads into Keystone Corner.

2. Keystone Corner 5.8
Stem, jam and wiggle your way to the top.

3. Copper Penny 5.10a
Cash in on this steep crack on beautifully bullet rock.

4. Five and Dime 5.10d
Climb the steep, continuous, straight-in hand crack. One of the best pitches around.

5. Whack and Dangle 5.11a
The steep right-leaning corner.

MOJO TOOTH AREA

  This area, located directly above the Hwy120/Hwy140 junction, hosts a good number of routes with incredible variety. Park at the dirt pullout at the junction and hike straight uphill from the east end of the parking lot to the crag. To access Mojo Tooth Right, hike above the left side, then traverse east and scramble to the bottom of Bad News Bombers.

LEFT SIDE

1. Unknown 5.10
Climb the far left route past a line of bolts.

2. Subatomic 5.11d
Head along the line of bolts through a crux roof section.

3. Unnamed 5.7
Climb the chimney into the flake.

4. Fluke 5.9
The bomber crack just right of 3.

5. Tongue And Groove 5.12a
Climb the steep double crack system.

6. Scratch and Sniff 5.12a
The diminishing crack right of Tongue And Groove.

RIGHT SIDE

7. New Traditionalist 5.10b
Climb up the face angling left towards the crack, then follow the crack to the top.

8. Yankee Clipper 5.11b
The bolt line up the right side of the arete.

9. Cereal Killer 5.10a
Climb the four-inch lieback up to the sugary-sweet hand crack.

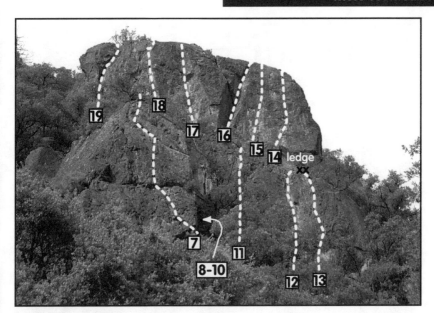

10. Figment 5.8
Climb the large dihedral right of Cereal Killer.
11. Grape Nuts 5.9
A great alternative to eating road gravel. Head up the left-facing crack right of Figment.
12. Eulogy 5.10a
Shoot up the crack past a roof in the center of the wall.
13. Mighty Crunchy 5.10d
Climb the tasty crack 15 feet right of Eulogy.
14. Yellow Peril 5.11b
Climb the steep bolt line on the right side of upper wall.
15. Golden Shower 5.12a
The steep bolt line left of Yellow Peril.
16. Natural End 5.9
Grunt your way up the flaring crack.
17. Jomo 5.11d
Blast up the left-facing bolted dihedral past the roof.
18. Deception 5.11
Climb the bolted dihedral left of Jomo.
19. Bad News Bombers 5.10a
Stem up the dihedral to the hand crack.

HIGHWAY STAR

This little cliff is located 1000 feet east of the Hwy140/Hwy120 junction. Park at the first big pullout east of the junction and at the 25 mph sign, hike a mere 100 yards to access awesome crack climbing.

1. Unknown 5.9
Climb up the dirty offwidth lieback. Have fun on this one.

2. Highway Star Variation 5.9
Climb the finger-sized lieback either up to the anchors of Highway Star or the previous route.

3. Highway Star 5.10
Start with a thin fingers lieback and continue up to steep hands.

LITTLE WING CLIFF

This cliff is easily approached by hiking along the Big Oak Flat Road that is accessed via the wood yard 0.2 mile west of El Capitan Meadow. A casual hike yields spectacular climbing in a fantastic setting.

1. Scuzz Ball 5.7
Climb the leftmost gray dihedral.

2. Squeeze and Tease 5.8
Oh behave! The big dihedral 20 feet right of Scuzz Ball.

3. L.D. Getaway 5.8
A beautiful hand crack that turns to fingers.

4. Andy Devine 5.7
Climb the big, junky right-facing dihedral up to a cleaner crack on the rightmost part of the wall.

(Bring two ropes for the following climbs)

5. He Can't Shout, Don't Hear You 5.7
Climb the left-facing dihedral just left of some fixed pins.

6. Gunks Revisited 5.11c
The small right-facing flake up to a left-angling roof and then cut left.

7. Honor Thy Father 5.10c
Skate up the very thin right-facing corner.

8. Leisure Time 5.10b
A route for those whose idea of an alpine start means sometime around noon. The beautiful left-angling finger crack left of The Riddler.

9. The Riddler 5.10a
Climb the ironically non-cryptic right-facing flake.

10. Little Wing 5.10d
Float up the left-facing thin crack to the right of The Riddler.

CAMP 4 WALL

 This little gem of a wall is found by hiking up the creekbed that runs into the west end of Camp 4 (Sunnyside) between the YOSAR (Yosemite Search and Rescue) site and Campsite 23. *Bring two ropes for this wall and rap from the top down to Rock Bottom's or Bottom Line's anchors. You can walk directly to the top of Buttocks and Cheek to set up an anchor. To access routes 1-3, rap from the anchors of Bottom Line down and left to the tree anchor atop Doggie Deviations.*

1. Doggie Diversions 5.9

Follow a 5.7 chimney up to a ledge and then up the awkward right-slanting large crack.

2. Doggie Deviations 5.9

Climb the double crack system 30 feet right of Doggie Diversions.

3. Doggie Deviations Variation 5.9

A really fun flake system just right of 2.

4. Bottom Line 5.11d

Climb the spectacular crack that shoots left up high into a 5.10 lieback. (The 5.11d moves can be eliminated by aiding through the bottom crux making this climb, as well as Rock Bottom, 5.10 and much more enjoyable.)

5. Rock Bottom 5.11d
Same start as for Bottom Line but head up and right at 2/3 height.
6. The Buttocks 5.9
Wrestle up the enormous, man-eating, right-facing chimney.
7. Cheek 5.10d
Head up the incredibly slabby finger crack to a crack-switching crux.

SWAN SLAB AREA
The Swan Slab Area is one of the most popular climbing areas in the Valley due to its easy access and fun, crowd-pleasing climbs. Swan Slab is located 100 yards east of Camp 4, directly across the road from Yosemite Lodge. The Swan Slab Area is subdivided into the three following areas:

PENTHOUSE CRACKS AREA

To set up the anchor for this area scramble left and up some dicey 4th class gullies, to gain the huge platform atop the large square block directly above the Penthouse Cracks. Here you'll find four bolts for anchors (bring 20 foot slings, as the bolts are set far back). *It is easiest to rappel down to the climbs after setting up the topropes. When you're finished, batman up the unclimbable slab and rappel off.*

1. Unnamed 5.10
Crank the greasy liebacks for 20 feet. Occasionally wet.
2. Unnamed 5.9
Climb the spectacular hand crack.
3. Unnamed 5.11
Jam the pin scars after the first move crux.
4. Unnamed 5.8
Lieback the fun hand crack. Also occasionally wet.

SWAN SLAB PROPER

5. Unnamed 5.7-5.8 (depending on variation)
Choose your own adventure on the slab below Penthouse Cracks.

6. Unnamed 5.3
Might be 5.3+. The corner just right of the slab.

7. Unnamed 5.8
Climb the short crack in the alcove 20 feet right of 6.

8. Unnamed 5.7
Climb the next crack right of 7.

9. Unnamed 5.8
The lieback crack just right of 8.

10. Unnamed 5.8
A few steps to the right is this dihedral.

GRANT'S CRACK AREA

To access the bolt anchors above Grant's Crack scramble up the gully directly left of the Oak Tree Flake.

11. Oak Tree Flake 5.6
Climb up the flake where the large oak tree is brushing up against the wall.

12. Grant's Crack 5.9
The cool double crack system right of Oak Tree Flake.

13. Unnamed 5.10
Dice up the discontinuous crack system right of Grant's Crack.

14. Unnamed 5.10+
The thin lieback crack right of 13.

SUNNYSIDE JAMCRACK AREA

This area is located just past Lower Yosemite Falls about 100 yards past the bridge directly beneath the falls and up the climbers trail. *If you can comfortably lead Sunnyside Jamcrack (5.7) and want to toprope hard but wonderful 5.10 cracks, then this is a good place for you.*

1. Sunnyside Jamcrack 5.7
The approach pitch to reach the anchors for all three routes. Enjoy stellar straight-in hand jams en route to the belay ledge with bomber bolts to toprope from.

2. Lazy Bum 5.10d
Get off your ass and climb the ever thinning crack just left of Sunnyside Jamcrack. High quality.

3. Bummer 5.10c
Start as with Lazy Bum but continue straight up past the neat rounded crystal hold to a near featureless crux.

CHURCH BOWL AREA

The Church Bowl Area lies on the road to the Ahwahnee Hotel approximately a 1/4 mile past Yosemite Village. Park in front of the large sign that says *Church Bowl* and head due north to the cliff. *To approach the anchors hike up and around 100 feet to the left of Deja Thorus and gain exposed ledges heading east. Continue to traverse exposed 4th class ledges to a tree 25 feet above the Uncle Fanny anchor tree and rap down to it. For routes 3-5 scramble east from the Uncle Fanny tree along the terrace to trees above the respective routes. Bring two ropes.*

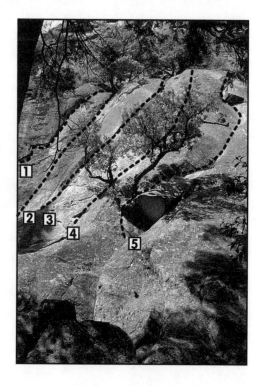

1. Deja Thorus 5.10a
A practice in strenuous flake pulling.

2. Uncle Fanny 5.7
Chimney climbing at its best.

3. Church Bowl Lieback 5.8
Climb the amazing hand crack and liebacks for 140 feet.

4. Pole Position 5.10
Unrivaled slab climbing between Church Bowl Lieback and Revival.

5. Revival 5.10a
Climb the super-fun finger crack to a roof crux.

INDIAN CAVE BOULDERS

This assortment of boulders is located near the Ahwahnee Hotel along the horse trail to Mirror Lake.

1. Space Invader 5.12a

This boulder sits directly across the road from the "Service Road Only" sign when you approach the Ahwahnee Hotel. This is a burly, incredibly overhanging 4-6 inch hand crack with bolt anchors at the top. Semi-visible from the road.

2. Pint Sized Boulder 5.10-5.12

Fathering a 5.10, a 5.11, and a 5.12, this boulder is conveniently located directly off the trail about 20 minutes from the hotel. There is a bolt anchor on top (reached from the backside) of the 5.12 from which to toprope from.

3. Pinkie Dick Boulder 5.10

This boulder is located about five more minutes past the Pint Sized Boulder roughly 100 yards off the trail to the north. Bring some gear to set up the 5.10 toprope problem.

Space Invader

5.12

5.10

5.11

3

4. Indian Cave Boulder 5.10

This boulder is also located directly off the trail approximately 25 minutes past the hotel and houses a fun 5.10 toprope. Bring 25 foot slings to tie off boulders and a tree at the rear of the boulder.

Indian Cave Boulder

5. Bad Ass Baby Boulder 5.11

A short but burly 5.11+ finger crack problem. Bring gear to set up the toprope. To access this boulder and the Bad Ass Momma Boulder hike 10 minutes beyond the Indian Cave Boulder. At a boulder with "climb" and an arrow chalked on it, head up a faint creekbed for 100 yards.

6. Bad Ass Momma Boulder 5.11

This mother is a gnarly 5.11+ offwidth problem located about 100 feet southeast of Bad Ass Baby. You can see this boulder faintly from the trail if you hike 5-10 minutes past the bathroom on the Mirror Lake Trail. Bring gear for setting up the anchor.

Bad Ass Baby

Bad Ass Momma

STAIRCASE FALLS AREA

Located directly behind the Curry Village cabins, this has three excellent toprope problems. To approach these climbs hike up the trail that parallels the creek bed between wooden cabins 71 and 72 for about five minutes. Upon arriving at the base of the wall, head west and you can't miss them.

1. Broken Circuit 5.12a
Climb the steep, left-angling crack with heinous finger locks and decent smears.

2. Circuit Breaker 5.11+
Climb the testy crack to the right of Broken Circuit.

3. Derelicts Delight 5.11+
Thirty feet to the right is another crack that should appeal to seedier individuals. Good finger locks down low lead to a roof crux up high.

Thanks go out to my my family for their everlasting support and guidance. I also owe a thanks to Tom Gage and Dargin Brasington for dealing with me while I was in Yosemite working on this book and to everyone else who has ever been around and helped climbing be a fun and positive experience.

-Rob Floyd

About the Author

Rob Floyd grew up three hours west of Yosemite National Park and has visited there for as long as he can remember. He began climbing on the sandstone cliffs of Castle Rock in California. After moving to Boulder, Colorado eleven years ago, Rob became a climbing addict.

In Boulder, Rob found his niche as a freelance writer and climbing guide. His work has been published in *Climbing, Rock and Ice* and *Freeskier Magazine*. When not writing about climbing, biking or skiing he can be found trying to improve his golf game. He is currently working on more Sharp End guidebooks, as well as a line of children's books and writing for an on-line golf publication.